W9-BKJ-813

THANKSGIVING

Stories and Poems

Edited by Caroline Feller Bauer
Illustrated by Nadine Bernard Westcott

HarperCollins*Publishers*

Thanksgiving
Stories and Poems
Text copyright © 1994 by Caroline Feller Bauer
Illustrations copyright © 1994 by Nadine Bernard Westcott, Inc.
"Supermarket Thanksgiving" copyright © 1994 by Caroline Feller Bauer
"There Once Was a Turkey Named Gus" copyright © 1994 by Marsha Cutler
"Images" and "Ballad of the *Mayflower*" copyright © 1994 by Linda G. Paulsen
"Thanksgiving Day," "The Thankful Mouse," and
"Working on the Turkey" copyright © 1994 by Grace Cornell Tall

Library of Congress Cataloging-in-Publication Data
Thanksgiving : stories and poems / edited by Caroline Feller Bauer;
illustrated by Nadine Bernard Westcott.
    p,   cm.
    Includes bibliographical references and index.
    Summary: A collection of stories, poems, and songs about Thanksgiving
Day, by such authors as Aileen Fisher, Jack Prelutsky, Eve Merriam, and
Yoshiko Uchida.
    ISBN 0-06-023326-5. — ISBN 0-06-023327-3 (lib. bdg.)
    1. Thanksgiving Day—Literary collections. [1. Thanksgiving Day—
Literary collections.]   I. Bauer, Caroline Feller.   II. Westcott, Nadine
Bernard, ill.
PZ5.T313   1994   93-18631
810.8'033—dc20   CIP
                                                            AC

4   5   6   7   8   9   10
❖

ACKNOWLEDGMENTS

Every effort has been made to trace ownership of all copyrighted material and to secure the necessary permissions to reprint these selections. In the event of any questions arising as to the use of any material, the editor and the publisher, while expressing regret for any inadvertent error, will be happy to make the necessary corrections in future printings. Thanks are due to the following for permission to reprint the selections below:

Curtis Brown, Ltd., for "The Skeleton Walks," from *One Winter Night in August*. Copyright © 1975 by X. J. Kennedy. / The Estate of Yoshiko Uchida, for "Autumn Walk" and "Bird Holiday." Copyright © 1985 by Yoshiko Uchida. / Marsha Cutler, for "There Once Was a Turkey Named Gus." Copyright © 1994 by Marsha Cutler. / Dell Books, a division of Bantam Doubleday Dell Publishing Group, Inc., for "Chester" from *Fables You Shouldn't Pay Any Attention To* by Florence Parry Heide and Sylvia Van Cleif. Copyright © 1978 by Florence Parry Heide and William C. Van Cleif III. / Greenwillow Books, a division of William Morrow & Company, Inc., for "The Thanksgiving Day Parade" from *It's Thanksgiving* by Jack Prelutsky. Text copyright © 1982 by Jack Prelutsky. / Greenwillow Books, a division of William Morrow & Company, Inc., for "I'm Thankful" from *The New Kid on the Block* by Jack Prelutsky. Text copyright © 1984 by Jack Prelutsky / HarperCollins Publishers, for "To Friendship" from *Under the Sunday Tree* by Eloise Greenfield. Text copyright © 1988 by Eloise Greenfield. / HarperCollins Publishers, for "All in a Word" from *Skip Around the Year* by Aileen Fisher. Copyright © 1967 by Aileen Fisher. / HarperCollins Publishers, for "Thanksgiving Dinner" from *In One Door and Out the Other* by Aileen Fisher. Copyright © 1969 by Aileen Fisher. / Bobbi Katz, for "A Thanksgiving Thought." Copyright © 1978. Used by permission of the author, who controls all rights. / J. Patrick Lewis, for "November." Copyright © 1994 by J. Patrick Lewis. / Morrow Junior Books, a division of William Morrow & Company, Inc., for "Thanksgiving" from *DeDe Takes Charge!* by Johanna Hurwitz. Text copyright © 1984 by Johanna Hurwitz. / Linda G. Paulsen, for "Images" and "Ballad of the *Mayflower*." Copyright © 1994 by Linda G. Paulsen. / G. P. Putnam's Sons, for "The Little Girl and the Turkey" from *All Together* by Dorothy Aldis. Copyright 1925–1928, 1934, 1939, 1952, copyright renewed © 1953–56 by Dorothy Aldis, © 1980 by Roy E. Porter. / Marian Reiner, for "Giving Thanks Giving Thanks" from *Fresh Paint* by Eve Merriam. Copyright © 1986 by Eve Merriam, published by Macmillan Publishing Company. / Grace Cornell Tall, for "Thanksgiving Day," "The Thankful Mouse," and "Working on the Turkey." Copyright © 1994 by Grace Cornell Tall.

FOR HILARY AND CHRIS:
*You don't need wishbones
anymore. Congratulations!*
—CFB

FOR BECKS,
*who I am thankful for
every day
Love, Mom*

Contents

AUTHOR'S NOTE

I do, therefor, invite my fellow citizens in every part of the United States . . . to set apart and observe the last Thursday of November next as a day of thanksgiving and praise to our beneficent Father who dwelleth in the heavens.

With this proclamation in 1863, President Abraham Lincoln established our national holiday of Thanksgiving.

The roots of this holiday probably began with America's first settlers. In 1621 and 1623 the Pilgrims and the Wampanoag Indians joined together to celebrate the Pilgrims' first successful harvests. They danced and played games and feasted on roast turkey, venison, fish, corn bread, and dried fruits.

Our celebrations today are not that different. There are parades and football games. And then friends and family gather together to feast on turkey, stuffing, mashed potatoes, cranberry sauce, and pumpkin pie.

But the holiday is less about what you eat than about how you feel. It is a day to be grateful for all the good things in your life and a perfect opportunity to tell people how much you love them. So hug your parents, be nice to your little sister, pull up a chair, and pass the stuffing.

Happy Thanksgiving!

THANKSGIVING
Stories and Poems

All in a Word

AILEEN FISHER

T for time to be together,
   turkey, talk, and tangy weather.

H for harvest stored away,
   home, and hearth, and holiday.

A for autumn's frosty art,
   and abundance in the heart.

N for neighbors, and November,
   nice things, new things to remember.

K for kitchen, kettles' croon,
   kith and kin expected soon.

S for sizzles, sights, and sounds,
   and something special that abounds.

That spells THANKS—for joy in living
   and a jolly good Thanksgiving.

Bird Holiday

YOSHIKO UCHIDA

There was a
noisy conference
of birds
outside my window
today.

Robins and linnets,
bushtits and sparrows,
and birds I didn't
even know.

They fluttered
and chirped
and took turns
nibbling at
my berry bush.

They made quite
a racket, they did.

I wonder how
they knew
it was
Thanksgiving,

Exactly the
right day
to gather
in flocks
to eat and
chatter and
make a lot of
noise
and then
fly away.

A Thanksgiving Thought

BOBBI KATZ

The day I give thanks for having a nose
Is Thanksgiving Day, for do you suppose
That Thanksgiving dinner would taste as good
If you couldn't smell it? I don't think it would.
Could apple pies baking—turkey that's basting
Not be for smelling? Just be for tasting?
It's a cranberry-cinnamon-onion bouquet!
Be thankful for noses on
Thanksgiving Day.

The Skeleton Walks

X. J. KENNEDY

Right after our Thanksgiving feast
Our turkey's bones went hobblin'
To Joan the wicked witch's house
To be her turkey goblin.

Ballad of the *Mayflower*

LINDA G. PAULSEN

There was a ship, *Mayflower* by name; Hey, Ho—
Took a trip, she crossed the main; Hey, Ho—
Full of people seeking peace,
Praying for freedom to increase;
Hey, Ho, Dee-o, Dee-o!

The Pilgrims came to Plymouth Rock; Hey, Ho—
Simple people, sturdy stock; Hey, Ho—
To be free they crossed the sea,
Thanked the Lord on bended knee;
Hey, Ho, Dee-o, Dee-o!

They planted corn the Indian way; Hey, Ho—
Every morn till end of day; Hey, Ho—
Worked and weeded to grow their crops,
Foods they needed till harvest stops;
Hey, Ho, Dee-o, Dee-o!

Now when the crops were gathered in; Hey, Ho—
A dinner party did begin; Hey, Ho—
Pilgrims, Indians, pumpkin pie,
Turkey, venison, corn, oh my!
Hey, Ho, Dee-o, Dee-o!

Bet you thought my song was done; Hey, Ho—
But I've really just begun; Hey, Ho—
Ever since that autumn day,
Thanksgiving has been here to stay.
Hey, Ho, Dee-o, Dee-o!

Thanksgiving Day

DOROTHY CANFIELD FISHER

A new girl came into the Winthrop Avenue public school about the beginning of November, and this is how she looked to the other boys and girls in the seventh grade. She couldn't understand English, although she could read it enough to get her lessons. (This was a small public school in a small inland American town where they seldom saw any foreigners, and people who couldn't speak English seemed outlandish.) She wore the queerest looking clothes you ever saw, and clumping shoes and great, thick, woolen stockings. (All the children in that town, as in most American towns, dressed exactly like everybody else, because their mothers mostly bought their clothes at Benning and Davis' department store on Main Street.) Her hair wasn't bobbed and curled, neither a long nor short bob; it looked as though her folks hadn't ever had sense enough to bob it. It was done up in two funny-looking pig-tails. She had a queer expression on her face, like nothing anybody had ever seen—kind of a smile and

11

yet kind of offish. She couldn't see the point of wise-cracks but she laughed over things that weren't funny a bit, like the way a cheer leader waves his arms. She got her lessons *terribly* well (the others thought somebody at home must help her more than the teachers like), and she was the dumbest thing about games—didn't even know how to play duck-on-a-rock or run-sheep-run. And queerest of all, she wore *aprons*! Can you beat it!

That's how she looked to the school. This is how the school looked to her. They had come a long way, she and her grandfather, from the town in Austria where he had a shop in which he repaired watches and clocks and sold trinkets the peasant boys bought for their sweethearts. Men in uniforms and big boots had come suddenly one day—it was in vacation and Magda was there and had smashed in the windows of the shop and the showcase with the pretty things in it, and had thrown all the furniture from their home in back of the shop out into the street and made a bonfire of it. And although Grandfather had not said a word to them, they had knocked him down, and hit him with their sticks till his white hair was all wet and scarlet with blood. Magda had been hiding in a corner and

12

saw this; and now, after she had gone to sleep, she sometimes saw it again and woke up with a scream, but Grandfather always came quickly to say smilingly, "All right, Magda child. We're safe in America with Uncle Harry. Go to sleep again."

He had said she must not tell anybody about that day. "We can do something better in the New World than sow more hate," he said seriously. She was to forget about it if she could, and about the long journey afterwards, when they were so frightened, and had so little to eat; and, worst of all, when the man in the uniform in New York thought for a minute that something was wrong with their precious papers, and they might have to go back. She tried not to think of it, but it was in the back of her mind as she went to school every day, like the black cloth the jewelers put down on their counters to make their pretty gold and silver things shine more. The American school (really a rather ugly old brick building) was for Magda made of gold and silver, shining bright against what she tried to forget.

How kind the teachers were! Why, they *smiled* at the children. And how free and safe the children acted! Magda simply loved the sound of their chatter on the playground, loud and gay and not afraid even when the teacher stepped out for something. She did wish she could understand what they were saying. She had studied English in her Austrian school, but this swift birdlike twittering didn't sound a bit like the printed words on the page. Still, as the days went by she began to catch a word here and there, short ones like "down" and "run" and "back." And she soon found out what *hurrah!* means, for the Winthrop Avenue School made a specialty of mass cheering and every grade had a cheer leader, even the first-graders. Magda thought nearly everything in America was as odd and funny as it was nice. But the cheer leaders were the funniest with their bendings to one side and the other and then jumping up straight in the air till both feet were off the ground.

But she loved to yell, "Hurrah!" too, although she couldn't understand what they were saying!

This is what they were saying—at least the six or seven girls who tagged after Betty Woodworth. Most of the seventh-graders were too busy studying and racing around at recess time to pay much attention to the queer new girl. But some did. They used to say, "My goodness, look at that dress! It looks like her grand-mother's—if she's got one."

"Of all the dumb clucks. She doesn't even know enough to play squat tag. My goodness, the first-graders can play *tag*."

"My father told my mother this morning that he didn't know why *our* country should take in all the dis-agreeable folks that other countries can't stand any more."

"She's Jewish. She must be. Everybody that comes from Europe now is Jewish. We don't want our town all filled up with Jews!"

"My Uncle Peter saw where it said in the paper we ought to keep them out. We haven't got enough for ourselves, as it is."

Magda could just catch a word or two, "country" and "enough" and "uncle." But it wouldn't be long now, she thought happily, till she could understand everything they said, and really belong to seventh grade.

About two weeks after Magda came to school Thanksgiving Day was due. She had never heard of Thanksgiving Day, but since the story was all written out in her history book she soon found out what it meant. She thought it was perfectly lovely! She read the story of the Pilgrim Fathers and their long hard trip across the ocean (she knew something about that trip) and their terrible first winter, and the kind Indian whose language they couldn't understand, who taught them how to cultivate the fields, and then—oh, it was poetry, just *poetry*, the setting aside of a day forever and forever, every year, to be thankful that they could stay in America! How could people (as some of the people who wrote the German textbooks did) say that Americans didn't care about anything but making money? Why here, more than three hundred years after that day, this whole school and every other school, everywhere all over the country, was turning itself upside down to celebrate with joy their great-grandfathers' having been brave enough to come to America and to stay here, even though it was hard, instead of staying in

Europe, where they had been so badly treated. (Magda knew something about that, too.)

Everybody in school was to do something for the celebration. The first-graders had funny little Indian clothes, and they were going to pretend to show the second-graders (in Puritan costumes) how to plant corn. Magda thought they were delightful, those darling little things, being taught already to be thankful that they

could go on living in America. Some grades had songs, others were going to act in short plays. The children in Magda's own seventh grade that she loved so, were going to speak pieces and sing. She had an idea all her own, and because she couldn't be sure of saying the right words in English she wrote a note to the teacher about it. She would like to write a thankful prayer (she could write English pretty well now), and learn it by heart and say it, as her part of the celebration. The teacher, who was terrifically busy with a bunch of boys who were to build a small "pretend" log-cabin on the stage, nodded that it would be all right. So Magda went away happily to write and learn it by heart.

"Kind of nervy, if you ask me, of that little Jew girl to horn in on our celebration," said Betty.

"Who asked her to come to America, anyhow?" said another.

"I thought Thanksgiving was for *Americans!*" said another.

Magda, listening hard, caught the word "American" and her face lighted up. It wouldn't be long now, she thought, before she could understand them.

No, no, they weren't specially bad children, no

more than you or I—they had heard older people talking like that—and they gabbled along, thoughtlessly, the way we are apt to repeat what we hear, without considering whether it is right or not.

On Thanksgiving Day a lot of those grown-ups whose talk Betty and her gang had been repeating, had come, as they always did, to the "exercises." They sat in rows in the assembly room listening to the singing and acting of the children and saying "the first-graders are too darling," and "how time flies," and "can you believe it that Betty is up to my shoulder now, seems like last week she was in the kindergarten."

The tall principal stood at one side of the platform and read off the different numbers from a list. By and by he said, "We shall now hear a prayer written by Magda Bensheim, and spoken by her. Magda has been in this country only five weeks and in our school only three."

Magda came out to the middle of the platform, a bright, striped apron over her thick, woolen dress, her braids tied with red ribbons. Her heart was beating fast. Her face was shining and solemn. She put her hands together and lifted them up over her head and said to God, "Oh thank you, thank you, dear God, for letting me come to America and nowhere else, when Grandfather and I were driven from our home. I learned out of my history book that Americans all came to this country just how Grandfather and I come, because Europe treat them wrong and bad. Every year they gather like this—to remember their brave grandfathers who come here so long ago and stay on, although they had such hard times. American hearts are so faithful and true that they forget never how they were all refugees, too, and must thankful be that from refugees they come to be American citizens. So thanks to you, dear, dear God, for letting Grandfather and me come to live in a country where they have this beautiful once-a-year Thanksgiving, for having come afraid from Europe to be here free and safe. I, too, feel the same beautiful thank-you-God, that all we Americans say here today."

Magda did not know what is usually said in English at the end of a prayer, so did not say anything when she finished, just walked away back where the other girls of her class were. But the principal said it for her—after he had given his nose a good blow and wiped his eyes. He looked out over the people in the audience and said in a loud, strong voice, "Amen! I say Amen, and so does everybody here, I know."

And then—it was sort of queer to applaud a prayer—they all began to clap their hands loudly.

Back in the seventh-grade room the teacher was saying, "Well, children, that's all. See you next Monday. Don't eat too much turkey." But Betty jumped up and said, "Wait a minute, Miss Turner. Wait a minute, kids. I want to lead a cheer. All ready?

"Three cheers for Magda!

"Hip! Hip!"—she leaned 'way over to one side and touched the floor and they all shouted, "Hurrah!"

She bent back to the other side, "Hurrah!" they shouted.

She jumped straight up till both feet were off the ground and clapped her hands over her head and "Hurrah!" they all shouted.

The wonderful moment had come. The curtain that had shut Magda off from her schoolmates had gone. "Oh! Ach!" she cried, her eyes wide. "Why, I understood every word. Yes, now I can understand American!"

The Little Girl and the Turkey

DOROTHY ALDIS

The little girl said
As she asked for more:
"But what is the Turkey
Thankful for?"

The Thanksgiving Day Parade

JACK PRELUTSKY

Thanksgiving Day is here today,
the great parade is under way,
and though it's drizzling quite a bit,
I'm sure that I'll see all of it.

Great balloons are floating by,
cartoon creatures stories high,
Mickey Mouse and Mother Goose,
Snoopy and a mammoth moose.

Humpty Dumpty, Smokey Bear
hover in the autumn air,
through the windy skies they sway,
I hope that they don't blow away.

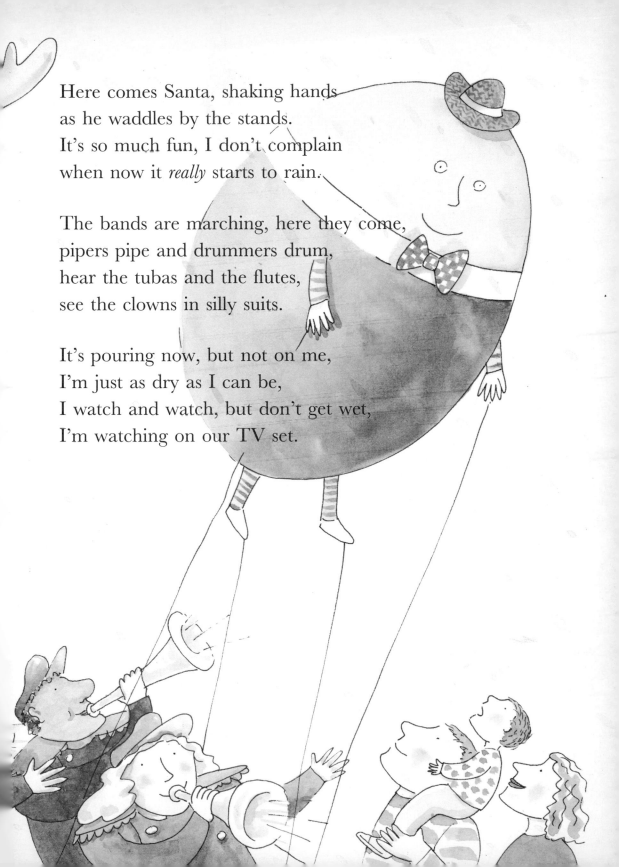

Here comes Santa, shaking hands
as he waddles by the stands.
It's so much fun, I don't complain
when now it *really* starts to rain.

The bands are marching, here they come,
pipers pipe and drummers drum,
hear the tubas and the flutes,
see the clowns in silly suits.

It's pouring now, but not on me,
I'm just as dry as I can be,
I watch and watch, but don't get wet,
I'm watching on our TV set.

Thanksgiving Day

GRACE CORNELL TALL

Clasp the hands,
Bow the head,

Ask the Lord
To bless the bread.

Pull the chair
Up to the table,

Eat no more
Than you are able.

Keep your elbows
Off the mats;

Save the leavings
For the cats.

(Ruff, who goes
From chair to chair,

Is getting much more
Than his share!)

Pass the dishes,
Help your mother.

Be sweet and good
To one another.

Then for this day,
Serene, unprankful,

We, your parents,
Will be thankful.

Thanksgiving

JOHANNA HURWITZ

The weekend had gotten off to a great start, and DeDe's spirits had stayed high until just before it was time for her to go home. That's when Mr. Rawson had told her that he had to leave on another business trip to California. She would not be able to spend her next scheduled weekend with him. And worst of all, that weekend was Thanksgiving.

Walking to school with Aldo on Monday morning, DeDe looked at the kindergarten windows. They were decorated with cutouts of turkeys that the little children had made.

"I wish I was back in kindergarten drawing turkeys again," DeDe said. Kindergarten was B.D. Before the Divorce.

"Hey," said Aldo. "You don't think I would hang around with a little kid in kindergarten, do you?"

DeDe shrugged miserably.

"So what's your father going to do in California?" Aldo asked.

"His company is opening a new office, and he's going there to arrange things. I wish Thanksgiving was over already," DeDe sighed. "I'm tired of looking at those old paper turkeys."

"Oh, well," said Aldo. "You'll soon be seeing Christmas decorations instead. They go up the second Thanksgiving is over."

DeDe nodded. She wondered where she would spend Christmas vacation. That was an even longer holiday than Thanksgiving.

"Maybe you could have Thanksgiving dinner at my house?" Aldo offered.

DeDe shook her head. She always enjoyed eating at Aldo's house, but Thanksgiving was a family holiday. She didn't want to spend it with someone else's family. "My mother and I will do something special," said DeDe. "Thanks anyhow."

There was still a week until Thanksgiving. DeDe waited to see what her mother would suggest. But when she didn't say anything, DeDe asked, "Could we plan a Thanksgiving dinner here and have company?"

"Oh, no," said Mrs. Rawson. "I still remember my last attempt at playing hostess."

"Could Grandma and Grandpa come?" asked DeDe. That would make the holiday really special.

"You've forgotten that they went to Florida. They rented an apartment there until March."

DeDe had forgotten. "Then it's just you and me," she said sadly.

"It could be worse," said Mrs. Rawson. "Before it was just me, and now I've got you."

DeDe looked at her mother. She hadn't asked herself if her mother would mind if she had gone off to visit her father. And she really hadn't thought about what her mother would do all alone on Thanksgiving.

"I know," said Mrs. Rawson. "Let's have dinner at a restaurant."

DeDe had always wondered what kind of people ate in restaurants on Thanksgiving. Orphans? Divorced people? People without any family or friends? It would probably be awful. Of course, she admitted, if she had been with her father she would almost certainly have eaten in a restaurant. But somehow that was different. DeDe didn't expect her father to cook his own holiday turkey.

"I don't want to eat out," DeDe pouted. "You

always make me order the kiddie specials. I don't want the Humpty Dumpty Dinner or the Bo Peep Platter for Thanksgiving."

"Of course not," agreed Mrs. Rawson. "You can order anything you want."

That was their plan for the holiday. But DeDe was not happy about it.

On Thanksgiving morning, she watched the big parade on television. She sat on the floor with her dog, Cookie, by her side and wondered what was wrong. She had watched the parade every year since she was a baby, but today something wasn't right. It didn't feel

like Thanksgiving at all. "I guess I'm getting too old to watch this," she told Cookie as she switched the dial on the TV, trying without success to find something else.

"It doesn't feel like Thanksgiving," DeDe complained to her mother.

Her mother nodded. "It's the smell."

"What smell?"

"This is the first year that we don't have a turkey roasting in the oven. The house doesn't smell like Thanksgiving," Mrs. Rawson explained. "We should invent a spray. You know how they sell rose and lemon deodorant sprays to make your house smell good. We should invent a turkey spray for people who don't roast a turkey on Thanksgiving. We could make a fortune."

But it wasn't just the smell that was wrong, DeDe knew. It was the absence of her father. This was the first Thanksgiving A.D. It wasn't something to be thankful about.

DeDe had an idea and went to the telephone. Quickly, she dialed her father's apartment in the city. The phone rang two times before there was a click and she heard her father's voice. "Hello. This is Henry Rawson. I am not at home at the moment, but I will return your call as soon as possible. At the signal, please leave your name, phone number, and a brief message. You will have twenty seconds."

DeDe sniffed and blinked her eyes. She had thought that hearing her father's voice would make her feel better. But it just made her feel worse. She hung up without saying anything. It didn't really matter. He wouldn't be home for another full week.

Mrs. Rawson had made a reservation at the Homestead Restaurant for two o'clock. At one, DeDe took off her jeans and started to put on her velvet party dress. She felt silly putting on a fancy dress to eat with her mother. She went into her mother's bedroom and saw that she was putting on her silk print dress.

"Look," her mother said proudly. "All those salads have helped me lose weight. This dress never fit so well before."

DeDe shrugged. Even though she had once been concerned about her mother getting fat, she was feeling too sorry for herself to care about that now.

She looked down at Cookie, who had been following her around. "I want Cookie to eat with us," she told her mother.

"The Homestead would never be the same," said Mrs. Rawson. "You know dogs aren't allowed in restaurants."

"Cookie isn't just a dog. She's family. And this is a family holiday," DeDe sulked. "If she can't come with us, I don't want to go."

"Maybe we can bring home a treat for her," offered Mrs. Rawson. "A doggie bag."

"I think a whole family should be together on a holiday," said DeDe. "It isn't right to leave Cookie here alone."

"Cookie doesn't know it's a holiday. She's probably wondering why you are home from school."

"I don't care. I want her to come with us," said DeDe.

"Cookie is staying home," said Mrs. Rawson firmly. "You and I are going out. Now that's final."

DeDe started to sob. "Cookie, you know I love you even if I go away."

"DeDe, stop making a soap opera out of this," warned Mrs. Rawson. She handed DeDe a tissue for her nose. "Let's go or we'll miss our reservation."

DeDe slumped down in the front seat of the car.

She didn't want any dinner at the Homestead. In the Pilgrims' day, animals and people all lived together and they ate together, too.

"You must be very hungry," said Mrs. Rawson as they drove along. "You hardly had any breakfast at all."

"I'm not hungry," DeDe growled.

After that Mrs. Rawson kept her eyes on the road. The Homestead parking lot was almost full, but there was a space near the front. Mrs. Rawson slowly edged into it, but she didn't allow enough room on the right side.

"Oh, dear," Mrs. Rawson sighed. She backed out slowly and tried to readjust her angle before pulling in.

Her mother pulled into and out of the space three times before she was finally able to make it. "Dad would have just zipped into this space," DeDe told her mother as she got out of the car.

"What can I tell you? I'm not perfect," snapped Mrs. Rawson.

"You can say that again," said DeDe. She was feeling angry, and angry words kept coming out of her mouth.

Mrs. Rawson didn't say anything. "What are you going to order?" she asked DeDe after they were seated.

DeDe looked down at the menu. "I'll take a broiled lobster."

"For Thanksgiving dinner?" asked Mrs. Rawson. "The Pilgrim fathers didn't eat lobster."

"I don't care about the Pilgrim fathers. My father eats lobster, and I want one, too."

"It's the most expensive dish on the menu. Are you sure you wouldn't prefer turkey?"

"You promised I could have anything I wanted,"

DeDe reminded her mother.

"Yes," agreed her mother. "I'd forgotten that you've developed such expensive tastes."

A family was seated across from the Rawsons: a mother, a father, a boy of seven, a girl of four, and two white-haired grandparents. DeDe looked at them enviously. They looked like a television commercial for soap or tomato sauce or something. She wished she were a part of that family.

DeDe leaned sideways in her chair, trying to hear what they were saying. Suddenly the mother turned to the grandmother and in a low voice hissed, "Oh, mother. Do be quiet." DeDe sat stunned. She felt betrayed. Those were not the words she had expected to hear from this "perfect family." Her eyes filled with tears for about the third time that afternoon. Did she sound that mean when she spoke to her mother?

The waitress came to their table. Mrs. Rawson ordered the turkey special for herself, and then she turned to DeDe.

"Me, too," DeDe whispered.

After the waitress left, DeDe said, "I can't bring lobster shells home for Cookie." Then she smiled at her mother. "I'm sorry, Mom," she said.

"So am I," her mother said. "It's not your fault that you're part of a modern statistic."

"What do you mean?" asked DeDe.

"More than half of all marriages end in divorce these days," her mother replied. "But children grow up anyway, and divorced people do go on with their lives—even if it may seem to you that I'm not doing such a good job of it right now. Everyone's life has its ups and downs," she said. "Sometimes it just takes a little longer to bounce up again." Her mother reached under the table and squeezed DeDe's hand. "Let's eat," she said as the waitress put the food on the table.

They had fruit cocktail, roast turkey and stuffing, candied sweet potatoes, string beans, and cranberry sauce. Mrs. Rawson turned down dessert, even though it came with the dinner. "My dress fits too well for me to risk it getting tight again. Besides," she said, "I am very full."

DeDe was full, too. But that was no reason to turn down apple pie with a scoop of chocolate ice cream.

"That was good," said DeDe.

"And no dishes to wash," said her mother, smiling.

When Mrs. Rawson paid the waitress, she said something to her quietly. The woman nodded. In a few minutes, she returned with a paper bag. DeDe peeked inside and saw two big steak bones for Cookie.

"Our dog is part of our family, so we didn't want to forget her today," said Mrs. Rawson.

"Her name is Cookie," said DeDe. "But she eats everything. Even stuffed cabbage."

DeDe took her mother's hand as they left the restaurant. The family at the next table was still eating. They looked like the perfect happy family. But looks could be deceiving. DeDe and her mother and Cookie were a family, too.

Turkey Dinner

ANONYMOUS

(sung to the tune of "Frère Jacques")

With spirit

arr. Ray Kimmelman

Tur - key din - ner, tur - key din - ner, Gath - er round, gath - er round,
Corn - bread muf - fins, chest - nut stuff - ing, Pud - din' pie, one foot high,

Who will get the drum - stick? Yum - my, yum - my drum - stick, All sit down, all sit down.
All of us were thin - ner Un - til we came to din - ner, Me - o - my, me - o - my.

I'm Thankful

JACK PRELUTSKY

I'm thankful for my baseball bat,
I cracked it yesterday,
I'm thankful for my checker set,
I haven't learned to play,
I'm thankful for my mitten,
one is missing in the snow,
I'm thankful for my hamsters,
they escaped a month ago.

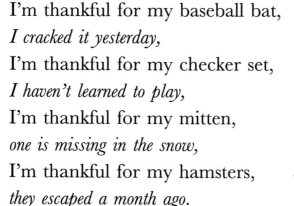

I'm thankful for my basketball,
it's sprung another leak,
I'm thankful for my parakeet,
it bit me twice last week,
I'm thankful for my bicycle,
I crashed into a tree,
I'm thankful for my roller skates,
I fell and scraped my knee.

I'm thankful for my model plane,
it's short a dozen parts,
I'm thankful for my target game,
I'm sure I'll find the darts,
I'm thankful for my bathing suit,
it came off in the river,
I'm thankful for so many things,
except, of course, for LIVER!

Thanksgiving Dinner

AILEEN FISHER

With company coming,
there's always *before*:
shine up the silver,
sweep up the floor,
corn and red peppers
to hang by the door,
salad to garnish
and water to pour,
sample the dressing
and gravy once more . . .
Listen!
They're coming!
Oh, run to the door!

The Thankful Mouse

GRACE CORNELL TALL

Though uninvited to my house,
A little mouse came in.
He passed an open water pail
And, curious, fell in.
Unhappily, he was a mouse
Who never learned to swim—
And there I was with fourteen guests
And no spare chair for him!
This happened on Thanksgiving Day,
And no one gave thanks more
Than this small mouse when, by his tail,
I pulled him from the water pail
And showed him to the door,
But not before I stuffed his vest
With crumbs of pie and turkey breast
To cheer him on his way.

45

Over the River

LYDIA MARIA CHILD

With galloping motion   arr. Ray Kimmelman

O - ver the ri - ver and through the wood, To grand - fa - ther's house we
O - ver the ri - ver and through the wood, To have _____ a first - rate
O - ver the ri - ver and through the wood, And straight through the barn - yard

go; _____ The horse knows the way To car - ry the sleigh Through the
play. _____ Hear the bells ring, _____ "Ting - a - ling - ding!" Hur -
gate. _____ We seem _____ to go Ex - treme - ly slow — It ___

white __ and drift - ed snow. ____ O-ver the ri-ver and | through the wood— Oh,
rah for Thanks-giv - ing Day! ____ O-ver the ri-ver and | through the wood, Trot
is __ so hard to wait! ____ O-ver the ri-ver and | through the wood— Now

how ____ the wind does blow! ____ It stings __ the toes And __
fast, ____ my dap - ple - gray! ____ Spring o - ver the ground Like a
grand-mo-ther's cap I spy! ____ Hur- rah for the fun! Is the

bites the nose, As o - ver the ground we go.
hunt - ing-hound! For this is Thanks-giv - ing Day!
pud - ding done? Hur- rah for the pump - kin - pie!

Chester

FLORENCE PARRY HEIDE

Chester was lazy.

Chester was the *laziest* turkey you ever heard of.

The other turkeys were always very busy doing whatever it is that all good turkeys should be doing.

But not Chester. He was too lazy.

He was too lazy to get out of bed.

"What would I do if I *did* get up?" he asked.

"Make your bed," said the other turkeys, who always made theirs.

"What's the use? I'm only going to get right back in it again," said Chester.

As you see, he was very lazy.

If he was inside, he was too lazy to go outside.

If he was outside, he was too lazy to go inside.

He was too lazy to go "gobble gobble." And all turkeys go "gobble gobble."

One chilly morning the farmer called the turkeys.

"Here turkey, turkey, turkey, turkey, turkey!" called the farmer.

All the other turkeys got ready to run to the farmer to see what he wanted. "Come on, Chester," said the other turkeys.

"I'm going to stay in bed," said Chester.

"You're so lazy, Chester. How will you know what the farmer wants?" asked the other turkeys.

"Come back and tell me," yawned Chester.

"Lazybones," said the other turkeys. They all ran to see what it was the farmer wanted.

The next morning, which was Thanksgiving morning, Chester looked around the empty barn. "It pays to be lazy," thought Chester, turning over for a little nap.

Thanksgiving Recipes

PUMPKIN PIE

1 cup sugar
1 tablespoon cornstarch
1 teaspoon cinnamon
$\frac{1}{2}$ teaspoon ginger
$\frac{1}{2}$ teaspoon nutmeg
$\frac{1}{2}$ teaspoon salt
1 15-ounce can of pumpkin
2 eggs, beaten
$1\frac{1}{2}$ tablespoons butter, melted
$1\frac{1}{2}$ cups milk
$\frac{1}{8}$ cup molasses
1 9-inch unbaked pie crust

Preheat the oven to 450°.

In a large bowl, sift together the sugar, cornstarch, cinnamon, ginger, nutmeg, and salt. Add the pumpkin and stir well. Next add the beaten eggs, melted butter, milk, and molasses, and stir until the mixture is smooth and well combined.

51

Pour the pumpkin filling into the unbaked pie crust and bake at 450° for 15 minutes. Then reduce the heat to 350° and continue to bake for another 50 minutes. The filling should seem set, and a knife inserted near the edge of the pie should come out clean when the pie is done.

Let cool, then refrigerate.

CRANBERRY SAUCE

2 cups sugar
1 ½ cups water
1 16-ounce package fresh cranberries

In a 2-quart saucepan over medium heat, bring the sugar and the water to a boil. Add the cranberries and heat until the mixture comes to a boil again. Then reduce the heat to low, cover, and simmer for 5 to 7 minutes, or until the cranberries pop. Serve warm, or chill to serve cold.

Autumn Walk

YOSHIKO UCHIDA

Crunch
        Crunch
Crunch
        Crunch

I love the sound
My feet can make
When the leaves
Turn red and
Yellow and brown,

And one dark night
The wind blows hard
Whirling them
Onto the walks
And streets
Where they tumble
And gather
In piles and drifts

54

Just waiting
For me and my
Marching feet
To come
Shuffling and
Scuffling and
Stomping
Up and down

Making a wonderful
Crunching sound

Crunch
        Crunch
Crunch
        Crunch

Me
And my feet
And the
Dry brown
Leaves.

Supermarket Thanksgiving

CAROLINE FELLER BAUER

Mrs. Lufkin works as a checker at Ben's Market. If you are in a hurry to buy your soda and get back to the Little League game, then you wouldn't want Mrs. Lufkin to check you out. She's slow! She checks the groceries quickly and makes change fast, but Mrs. Lufkin likes to talk. She holds up the checkout line to ask about your new baby brother or the new teacher at school.

Her favorite conversation opener is "What do you make with this?" She points to something in a shopping cart, and people start giving a cooking lesson right there in front of the cash register.

Everyone thinks that Mrs. Lufkin is a gourmet cook since she talks food all day. She is quite large, maybe even fat. However, I know that although Mrs. Lufkin loves to eat and talk, she isn't much of a cook. I know because Mrs. Lufkin is my mom. She says, "Why spend time cooking when you can spend the time eating?" Of course, since her hobby and job involves food,

57

she loves to collect recipes. "Someday you'll get married, David. I'll give you a book of recipes. I'll call it *Mom's Favorite Eating.*"

I used to be embarrassed listening to Mom ask questions about people's eating habits. Now I'm just as curious as she is.

"Oh, I see you're making piroshki today," she said to the Ukrainian woman who moved to town last year. We got to taste piroshki when Mrs. Manchev brought some to the market last week. At first I thought that they were apple turnovers. And I'm glad I didn't tell her that I hate onions, because they sure tasted good mixed with the spiced meat inside the dough. I could have eaten them all.

When the Korean man who lives down the street comes to the market, Mom asks, "Planning to make kimchi?"

I know Mom has never tasted kimchi, but she knows that the main ingredient is cabbage. Mr. Sung almost always has a head of cabbage in his cart.

"Nice mess of shrimp you have there. Are you fixing to make that jambalaya?"

The school-bus driver, Mr. Potter, nods. He is from

Louisiana, or someplace in the South. Sometimes his father, a widower, rides with him on the bus. He calls out the stops in a southern accent. The kids love it.

"Jambalaya sounds like the name of a band," I say, bagging the groceries.

"Jambalaya is music to the palate, David. The chili and cayenne pepper sing on your tongue," Mr. Potter says as I hand him his grocery sack.

Once I heard Mom say to Sharlene, the exchange student from Australia, "Going to make that dancer's dessert tonight?"

"Yes, Mrs. Lufkin. It's called Pavlova."

Pavlova was a famous ballet dancer, and a chef created the dessert to honor her. Mom feels sorry for dancers, though. "They are so thin, they must never eat a piece of pie or ice cream. I wonder if Pavlova ever had a piece of her own dessert?"

The owner and manager of Ben's is my dad. He never complains about Mom holding up the checkout line. He admires the way she talks to everyone.

"Edith," he says, "you're the friendliest person I have ever known. I could never start a conversation with a man just because he buys shrimp." Dad often finds a reason to stand by the cash register. He likes to hear about recipes too, since he is the cook in our family.

One day my mother noticed that Mr. Sung had bought only enough food for one person.

"My wife is visiting her family in Seoul. I'm cooking for myself this month," he explained.

Then it turned out that Sharlene's boyfriend, Roger, was coming from Down Under.

"I want to show him the real America," she said.

"I'm not sure what the real America is," said Mom, "but an American holiday is coming. You could make him a Thanksgiving dinner."

"But I don't know how to cook anything except Pavlova."

"I have a brilliant idea," said my mom. "The market is shut Thanksgiving Day. Why don't you and Roger join us for the holiday dinner? Ben will cook the traditional turkey, and he makes divine matzo-ball soup. You could make your Pavlova for the dessert. I'll invite Mr. Sung, too. His wife is out of town."

I said, "Can we fit that many people in our apartment?"

"The dinner doesn't have to be in our apartment. The Pilgrims had their dinner outside. It was a picnic."

"We can't have a picnic. It snowed last week."

"A dinner can be anywhere," insisted Mom. "It could be right here in our store."

"The store is big," said my Dad, "but where would we have a dinner? On the checkout counter?"

"We'll think of something. Meanwhile, who else can we invite?" Mom wondered.

"Mr. Potter and his father might want to come," Dad suggested. He knew there was no stopping my mom when she had a brilliant idea.

"Who else?"

Mom thought of a lot of other people who would be alone for Thanksgiving. "It's a family holiday," she said. "So everyone who can't be with their families can be a part of our family this Thanksgiving."

Our family got bigger and bigger as it got closer to Thanksgiving. Mrs. Manchev was coming and bringing her niece.

I invited my friend Paul and his mom. "We never have turkey. You can't have a big dinner for just two people," he told me.

Dad invited the Wertheim brothers. They sell us all our cleaning supplies. "They can contribute by

cleaning up," Dad said.

"How about Gertie? She's the one who buys all that dog food."

"Can we invite her dog, too?"

Finally the guest list was complete. Next we needed to decorate the store. In the market we sell Thanksgiving greeting cards showing fruit and nuts spilling from a horn of plenty. We didn't need to search very far for fruit and nuts. The dinner was going to be held between the frozen-food case and the produce stands.

"The frozen food will look like a mural. The fresh vegetables will look like they took hours to arrange," said Mom.

"They do take hours to arrange," laughed Dad. He is the produce manager, too.

"Should we use the paper plates that we sell?" I asked.

"Absolutely not," Mom said, horrified. "It's Thanksgiving. Time to use Great-Aunt Molly's china."

When Thanksgiving Day arrived, it seemed strange to be in the store on a holiday. We set up Paul's Ping-Pong table in the aisle with a card table on either end. The card tables were lower than the Ping-Pong table. "Good. A two-tiered table is much more interesting." said Mom. Gertie brought chairs from her church, and her dog in his own playpen.

Sharlene came early to help too. She put her Pavlova in the refrigerator section, next to the milk and butter. Her boyfriend, Roger, has the neatest accent.

"Most odd that it's fall here," he said. "It's spring in Perth."

He knew how to fold the napkins so that they looked like swans.

"I'm not going to use my swan. I'm going to save it forever," I said.

"David, if you're not going to use the cloth napkin, then get some of those Thanksgiving paper napkins from aisle eight. Might as well use them. They'll be on sale when we reopen tomorrow," Mom said.

When our guests, I mean, family, started to arrive, they each brought a dish they had made. The main dishes were lined up down the middle of the table.

It looked like a wonderful feast. But something was missing.

"We forgot candles," I said.

"Well, go over to aisle seven and get some candles and holders. Matches are on aisle three."

"If you forget something at this dinner, we don't have to send someone to the store to get it." Mr. Potter's dad smiled.

At last we were ready to eat. "Wait!" said Mr. Sung. "We need to say thank you to all our friends for this wonderful dinner. In our country we say *komapsumnida*."

"*Komapsumnida*, y'all," said Mr. Potter.

"*Komapsumnida!*" we all shouted.

We started with my father's matzo-ball soup. "My

grandmother's recipe," said Dad. "She left Poland before World War Two."

Then Dad carved the turkey and Mrs. Manchev passed around her piroshki. We had jambalaya, too. It was hot! I had to drink about a gallon of nam manao, the Thai limeade, to cool off my mouth. *"Komapsumnida,"* I said to Gertie, who had brought it. She had lived in Thailand when she was a little girl.

I was not looking forward to Mr. Sung's kimchi. Cabbage and vinegar is not my idea of a holiday dish. I didn't have to worry.

"I brought moon cakes," said Mr. Sung. "Our moon festival is over, but these are my favorite holiday treats."

"These cookies look just like a full moon, except for the almond on top. I'm going to eat that first," said Paul.

"Has everyone saved some room for dessert?" asked Mom. "I'm ready to taste Sharlene's Pavlova."

"David, would you and Paul go over to the butter case to get it?" asked Dad.

Roger was thrilled.

"Sharlene, I didn't know that you could cook!"

Sharlene blushed and said, "It's the only dish I know how to make. It was invented to honor the famous ballet dancer, and I've taken ballet lessons since I was six, so I thought I should know how to make it. My grandmother showed me how just before I came to the States."

"Who needs to know anything else?" said Roger. "It has all the food groups: sugar, egg whites for the meringue, then sugar, fruit, sugar, cream, and more sugar."

"Don't tease her," said Mom. "If Sharlene wants to learn how to cook, she can stand with me at the checkout counter and ask the customers how they cook all these delicacies."

"*Komapsumnida,*" said Sharlene.

"I couldn't eat another thing," said the famous chef Mrs. Lufkin. "But please pass the Pavlova. I want seconds."

Working on the Turkey

GRACE CORNELL TALL

Father buys it.
Mother cooks it.
Sally bastes it.
Johnny tastes it.
And little Elmer,
In his chair,
All he does is
Coo and stare.

There Once Was a Turkey Named Gus

MARSHA CUTLER

There once was a turkey named Gus.
Each November he raised a big fuss.
The feathers would fly,
He'd scream and he'd cry,
"My motto's December or bust."

70

Images

LINDA G. PAULSEN

Some people see the turkey
Roasted to a golden brown.
Some people think of families
That come from out of town.

Some remember fondly
That there's no school for the day,
And maybe one or two are glad
That Grandma comes to stay.

But when I think "Thanksgiving,"
I have some different wishes,
'Cause for me it usually means
Just stacks of dirty dishes!

Giving Thanks
Giving Thanks

EVE MERRIAM

Giving thanks giving thanks
for rain and rainbows
sun and sunsets
cats and catbirds
larks and larkspur

giving thanks giving thanks
for cows and cowslips
eggs and eggplants
stars and starlings
dogs and dogwood

giving thanks giving thanks
for watercress on river banks
for necks and elbows knees and shanks
for towers basins pools and tanks
for pumps and handles lifts and cranks

72

giving thanks giving thanks
for ropes and coils and braids and hanks
for jobs and jokes and plots and pranks
for whistles bells and plinks and clanks
giving giving giving *thanks*

Gobble Gobble Garland

HOW TO MAKE A THANKSGIVING DECORATION

To make a colorful Thanksgiving decoration, you will need:

• a long sheet of paper. The longer the sheet, the more turkeys will be dancing around your dining room. The paper should be about 5 inches high, so you could cut out strips of paper and tape them together to make a long garland. Try using construction paper, wrapping paper, newspaper, or adding-machine tape.
• a pencil
• a pair of scissors
• some markers or crayons

Fold your long sheet of paper accordion style as shown, making the folds about 4 inches wide.

Draw a turkey on the first fold, making sure its beak and tail feathers touch the sides of the folds. You

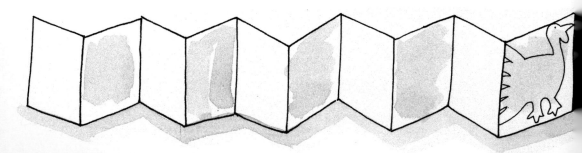

can trace the turkey on this page or draw your own.

Cut through the paper on the outline and then unfurl your gobble garland.

If you like, you can decorate your turkeys further with crayons or markers.

November

J. PATRICK LEWIS

The bottoms of autumn
Wear diamonds of frost;
The tops of the trees rue
The leaves that they've lost.

Red squirrels, busy packing
Oak cupboards for weeks,
Still rattle the branches
With seeds in their cheeks.

Gray clouds go on promising
Winter's first storm,
So we stay inside by
The stove to keep warm.

Home biscuits are baking,
The gravy is stirred,
Two pumpkin pies cool
By the thank-you bird.

To Friendship

ELOISE GREENFIELD

It's time for the party
and as we begin
let's do a sentimental
thing
let's lift our punch
to the bunch
(that's us)
we'll say that our
friendship is dear and
we'll promise to keep it from
year to year
and
this toast we'll repeat
each time we meet
and now, my friends—
let's eat

Something to Read

PICTURE BOOKS

Friendship's First Thanksgiving, by William Accorsi. Illustrated by the author. Holiday House. *A small dog who traveled on the* Mayflower *tells the story of the first Thanksgiving.*

An Old-Fashioned Thanksgiving, by Louisa May Alcott. Illustrated by Michael McCurdy. Holiday House. *In their parents' absence, the Bassett children attempt to prepare Thanksgiving dinner.*

Sometimes It's Turkey—Sometimes It's Feathers, by Lorna Balian. Illustrated by the author. Abingdon Press. *Mrs. Gumm and her cat raise a turkey to eat for Thanksgiving, but the turkey joins the feast as a guest.*

Arthur's Thanksgiving, by Marc Brown. Illustrated by the author. Little, Brown. *Who will play the part of the turkey in the Thanksgiving play?*

Three Young Pilgrims, by Cheryl Harness. Illustrated by the author. Bradbury Press. *Mary, Remember, and Bartholomew are Pilgrims settling in the new world.*

One Tough Turkey: A Thanksgiving Story, by Steven Kroll.

Illustrated by John Wallner. Holiday House. *Solomon Turkey does not want to be eaten at the first Thanksgiving.*

'Twas the Night Before Thanksgiving, by Dav Pilkey. Illustrated by the author. Orchard Books. *Children on a field trip save eight turkeys in a Thanksgiving version of "The Night Before Christmas."*

One Terrific Thanksgiving, by Marjorie Weinman Sharmat. Illustrations by Lilian Obligado. Holiday House. *Irving Morris Bear thinks only about food until his friends remind him of something more important.*

Thanksgiving at the Tappletons', by Eileen Spinelli. Illustrated by Maryann Cocca-Leffler. HarperCollins. *The entire family helps with the dinner, but nothing goes right.*

Fried Feathers for Thanksgiving, by James Stevenson. Illustrated by the author. Greenwillow. *Young Emma witch is determined to put on a memorable Thanksgiving dinner despite Dolores and Lavinia witch, who want to ruin the day.*

Thanksgiving Treat, by Catherine Stock. Illustrated by the author. Bradbury Press. *Everyone but the youngest has a job preparing Thanksgiving dinner.*

Turkey on the Loose!, by Sylvie Wickstrom. Illustrated by the author. Dial Press. *A turkey gets loose and runs through an apartment house.*

LONGER BOOKS

Silly Tilly's Thanksgiving Dinner, by Lillian Hoban. Illustrated by the author. HarperCollins. *Silly Tilly finally gets a dinner together.*

The Thanksgiving Treasure, by Gail Rock. Illustrated by Charles C. Gehm. Alfred A. Knopf. *Addie befriends a cranky old man.*

The Turkeys' Side of It: Adam Joshua's Thanksgiving, by Janice Lee Smith. Illustrated by Dick Gackenbach. HarperCollins. *Adam Joshua is disappointed in his part in the school play.*

POETRY

Merrily Comes Our Harvest In: Poems for Thanksgiving, edited by Lee Bennett Hopkins, illustrated by Ben Shecter. Harcourt, Brace. *A happy collection of poems.*

Thanksgiving Poems, selected by Myra Cohn Livingston. Illustrated by Stephen Gammell. Holiday House.

Original poems for the holiday.

It's Thanksgiving, by Jack Prelutsky. Illustrated by Marylin Hafner. Greenwillow. *Funny, irreverent poems.*

INFORMATIONAL BOOKS

The First Thanksgiving Feast, by Joan Anderson. Photographs by George Ancona. Clarion. *A photographic reenactment of the first Thanksgiving.*

Thanksgiving Magic, by James W. Baker. Art by George Overlie. Lerner. *Put on a magic show at your Thanksgiving feast.*

Happy Thanksgiving, by Carol Barkin and Elizabeth James. Illustrated by Giora Carmi. Lothrop, Lee & Shepard. *Ideas for things to make and do for Thanksgiving.*

Thanksgiving Day, by Gail Gibbons. Illustrated by the author. Holiday House. *A short history of the holiday and some ways we celebrate it.*

Cranberries, by William Jaspersohn. Photographs by the author. Houghton, Mifflin. *Where do the cranberries come from?*

The Dragon Thanksgiving Feast: Things to Make and Do, by Lorraine Leedy. Illustrated by the author. Holiday

House. *Arts and crafts ideas.*

Wild Turkey Tame Turkey, by Dorothy Hinshaw Patent. Photographs by William Muñoz. Clarion. *A survey of wild and domesticated turkeys.*

Autumn Festivals, by Mike Rosen. Bookwright Press. *Fall celebrations around the world.*

The Pilgrims of Plimoth, by Marcia Sewall. Illustrated by the author. Atheneum. *How the pilgrims lived and worked and feasted.*

High Ridge Gobbler: The Story of the American Wild Turkey, by David Stemple. Illustrated by Ted Lewin. Collins. *This is the turkey that probably was served at the first Thanksgiving.*

Index

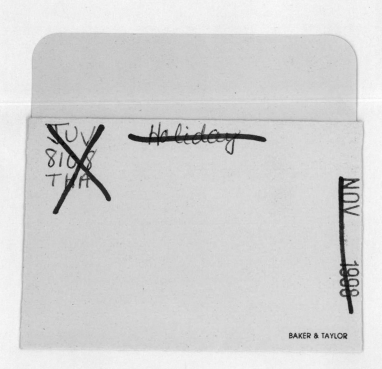